# THE LOYAL LIEUTENANT

How The Second-In-Command
Brings The CEO's Vision To Life

By Shirley Dalton

Published by Dalton Publishing, Newcastle, Australia

Copyright © 2022 Shirley Dalton

shirleydalton.com

Title: The Loyal Lieutenant: How The Second-In-Command Brings The CEO's Vision To Life

Author: Shirley Dalton

ISBN 978-0-6454025-1-3 (ebook)

ISBN 978-0-6454025-0-6 (pbk)

A catalogue record for this book is available from the National Library of Australia

**Disclaimer**: Any advice or information in this publication is of a general nature only and has not considered your personal needs or circumstances. Seek advice from a qualified professional to consider whether this information is appropriate for your needs or circumstances before making any business, financial or personal decisions.

**All rights reserved.** No portion of this book may be reproduced, stored in a retrieval system, or transmitted in any form without written permission of the author, except in the case of brief quotations within articles or reviews.

# Praise For The Loyal Lieutenant

It's one thing to have a visionary in your company. It's another thing to have a Second-In-Command (2IC) who's going to make the vision happen. In my opinion, the Second-In-Command is the most important person for a visionary. They allow the vision to come to life and for everyone part of that vision to benefit from it.

Shirley Dalton has worked ON my businesses as a consultant and IN my businesses as COO (Chief Operating Officer) next to me as CVO (Chief Vision Officer). Shirley has a knack for helping visionaries put their vision into words, then systems, then an org chart and then into functioning roles that everyone can feel connected to and bring to life.

It's beautiful to watch your vision come to life and for every stakeholder to benefit from being part of the business ecosystem you've created. That's what's happened to me, thanks to working with Shirley. Our businesses include the fastest growing buyers agency in Australia, Henderson Advocacy; a new real estate sales business owned and run by one of the top three agents in Australia for sales, Clarke & Co Estate Agents; a nationally recognised eight-figure real estate group of offices, PRD Presence; and Real Business Engine, the white label business behind these businesses that has so much demand for new partnerships we get to choose who we work with. I've known Shirley since 2005 and she's done it all, from small start-ups, to internationally listed companies and everything in between.

If you're aspiring to be the Second-In-Command of the next business to break through, scale and become an employer of choice, you need to buy two copies of this book. One to break apart and take copious amounts of notes on, and one to always keep with you. Shirley is the mentor you need. The lifelong lessons she brings to the table will save you a decade of trial and error.

*Mark Kentwell, 3x Winner of REB Real Estate Principal of the Year Australasian, Thought Leader of The Year Finalist 2022 and Chief Vision Officer PRD Presence, Henderson Advocacy and Real Business Engine*

"This is the next best thing to having Shirley come in and start documenting your procedures for you. And I know, having had her standing beside me and asking: "How come you do that? How come you do that?" This book will really open your eyes to a new way of thinking about your role and help you get an extra day a month of time, to do with as you please - like I did."

*Meg McNaughton, HR Lawyer*

"What you'll gain from this book is a new level of confidence. Shirley was the confidence I needed to tackle some demons I'd been struggling with for a long time. Not only professionally but personally too. For anyone like me, who is feeling unsure, I would say ignore those voices in your head, throw yourself in the deep end – you won't regret it!"

*Jessica McCreanor, Business Services Manager and Senior Accountant*

"Reading this book is like having Shirley on your team. I found that it made me come out of my shell more, speak my mind more confidently and give me the reassurance I needed to validate why I am in the role I am in at my workplace. I feel that implementing a lot of my learnings with my team at work has really made us strive and come together."

*Courtney Mathieson, Accounts Manager*


"Shirley will help you understand yourself, in order to become a great leader. I can hear Shirley's voice as she offers advice and support through the book. From Shirley, I've learned how to articulate what I see happening, how to listen better, how to get organised in my head and clear on actions, how to work out what to delegate, and how to understand staff and work in a productive way with each individual. This book will do the same for you too."

*Corlia Bunn, COO*

*To Ross, for being my Loyal Lieutenant.*

*I couldn't do the things I do without you.*

**Thank You**

# Acknowledgement

This book could never have been written without having had the wonderful opportunity to work with my awesome clients over the past 16 years. I am eternally grateful for their willingness to work with me, trust me and share some of their most vulnerable moments with me. I am honoured to count my clients as friends and family, many of whom have continued to work with me over many many years. Thank you!

I am also grateful for the many mentors and teachers I have had over the years as Ross and I travelled the world working with the best of the best and investing many hundreds of thousands of dollars into our own personal growth and development.

I am especially grateful to Kip McGrath and his late wife, Dagnija McGrath, from whom I learned so much about showing up authentically and doing what's required to create both an enduring and successful business and legacy for children all around the world.

And speaking of successful businesses and business owners, I am grateful for the opportunity to have worked very closely with Mark Kentwell over the years as he grew his business from humble beginnings in his early twenties to the juggernaut that it is today. It's a privilege to work with such visionary leaders.

And special mention to Kellie O'Brien for her constant support, encouragement and willingness to stay the distance on this ever changing journey with a Last Minute Lucy.

Without Kellie's organisational skills, award winning journalistic skills and constant accountability, this book would still be something on the "To Do" list. It takes a team to get stuff done and I am so grateful to my editor Kellie and designer Chrystie Hile for their valuable insights and ability to truly listen and nail the brief every single time. Thank you Kellie and Chrystie, couldn't have done it without you.

And of course, a special thanks to my husband Ross for his unwavering love and support over the past 30+ years, for always being there and saying "Yes" to the next idea and adventure without question. Love ya lots.

# CONTENTS

Foreword     11

Introduction     14

## SECTION 1 - SECOND-IN-COMMAND THE MOST IMPORTANT PERSON

**Chapter 1**
Putting On The Lieutenant's Jacket     17

**Chapter 2**
The Science of Business Freedom     23

**Chapter 3**
Why You Are So Needed and So Valuable     29

## SECTION 2 - 4 SIMPLE STEPS TO BUSINESS FREEDOM

**Chapter 4**
Step 1 – Map Your Processes     45

**Chapter 5**
Step 2 – Your Organisation Structure     57

Chapter 6

Step 3 – Role Clarity     63

Chapter 7

Step 4 – Scale and Grow (Procedures – the How)     71

## SECTION 3 – CUSTOMISE YOUR BUSINESS PROCESSES

Chapter 8

Use the Process and Customise to
Your Organisation     77

Chapter 9

Promote Yourself     85

# Foreword

In 1976, my late wife Dagnija and I founded Kip McGrath Education Centres with the simple ideology that, "Every child can learn, they just need to be taught properly."

By 2000, our original centre had become an international franchise organisation with 200 centres in Australia and internationally.

In August 2000, we recruited Shirley Dalton as franchise manager with the rather skimpy job description, "To liaise with the Australian franchisees and international master franchisees."

Shirley spent just a few weeks getting to know the business and developing an understanding of what was required of her. She spoke to franchisees and master franchisees to get a complete picture of where the business currently stood.

She also spent considerable time talking to me. She understood that if she was to be an effective leader in the organisation, then she had to understand where the entrepreneur wanted to head.

Very quickly Shirley and I had developed a trusting and respectful relationship. It enabled us to shake hands and seal a deal where I agreed to give her three years of management training and Shirley committed to five years of service. There were no written agreements, we didn't feel we needed any.

Within weeks Shirley began developing better systems and developing them in areas where we had none. This was a huge job because we had franchisees who could be difficult to manage because they paid for the business and believed they had special rights. We had master franchisees who had similar issues to franchisees and who were also many thousands of kilometres away. We also had an IT department and anybody who has had one understands that IT people have their own management issues.

Shirley was organised and conscientious. The highlight of these early days was that Shirley listened to the franchisees and master franchisees and was able to understand their issues. Once this was done, solutions could be found. She worked with our internal IT department to develop automated systems, saving time, money and mistakes.

Shirley had now become truly the number two and her job title was changed to Chief Operating Officer.

I enjoyed working with Shirley because she was highly intelligent and enthusiastic. As well as doing a great job, she was anxious to learn what I could teach her. During our time working together, the business grew to 550 centres in 20 countries. The company listed on the Australian Stock Exchange. Shirley continued to refine our systems to cope with the expanding business.

I was sad to lose her when she left to start her own consultancy business in October 2006 – Dalton Business Systems. However, I understood that Kip McGrath Education Centres was a stepping stone for her.

Shirley may have learned a lot from me, but I learned a lot from her. I currently help young people develop their businesses. The systems she taught me I'm now teaching others. The other thing that has been of enormous help to me is how to speak or write to people when you're not happy with them. "No 'You Statements', Kip" will forever remain in my head.

The Loyal Lieutenant: How The Second-In-Command Brings The CEO's Vision To Life is your guidebook if you're a senior leader in an organisation.

In this, Shirley shares what she's learned over the past three decades to help you accelerate your journey and save you from making the same mistakes she made.

Written in plain English with step-by-step instructions for how to streamline and systemise your operations, I can attest that Shirley's methodology works.

This book is for you if you're just starting your journey as a senior leader or if you're looking for practical ways to improve the efficiency and productivity of your business or section.

If you complete the assignments in the book, I am confident you too will become comfortable in your lieutenant's jacket. I know your CEO will be especially pleased to have the help and support to see his vision come to life.

I know I was.

Kip McGrath, Co-Founder Kip McGrath Education Centres
Newcastle, NSW
January 2022

# Introduction

Dear Second-In-Command,

This book was written especially for you.

In my experience as a former Chief Operating Officer and consultant to business owners, entrepreneurs, leaders and managers, I've found organisations get the best results when the CEO and the Second-In-Command team up.

Individually, you have exceptional yet complementary skills and attitudes. Typically, the CEO sees an opportunity and acts with speed. They have a vision, yet they can struggle to communicate this clearly and have little patience for details.

As the Second-In-Command, you're called upon to interpret the vision. It's your job to reverse engineer and develop an action plan and strategy to achieve the results. You're in charge of operations, and you know what's going on at any given time. Your knowledge, skill and attention to detail is mission critical. Without you, chaos and inefficiency reign.

You understand and can speak both languages; that of the visionary CEO and the practicality of the team. You understand that the more efficient you and the team are, the more the boss can step aside and let you get on with the job. This gives you more time, more money, more authority, and ultimately more freedom.

Running an efficient operation is a true win/win/win. You win, your boss wins and the team wins – not to mention the customers.

This book has been designed to acknowledge how important your role is within the organisation, and to give you the tools that will help you create even more order and structure in the business.

If you choose to take on the role of champion and accept the responsibility for implementing the four critical steps, you'll enjoy the immense sense of achievement that comes with knowing and appreciating the difference you make, not to mention more time, more money and even more authority.

Yours is a unique set of skills – let's make the most of them.

Shirley Dalton

Newcastle, NSW, Australia

# SECTION 1

## SECOND-IN-COMMAND
## THE MOST IMPORTANT PERSON

---

## Chapter 1
## Putting On Your Lieutenant's Jacket

"Your mother is in the hospital," Dad said down the phone line. My uncle had just passed away and my mother, who was battling breast cancer, was tasked with cleaning his house. Having overdone it, she now had oedema in her arm, which had caused serious swelling.

"When did she go to hospital?" I asked.

Dad's voice changed pitch. "Oh... yesterday."

I hit the roof. It was 9pm on a Friday and we were living in Brisbane, Queensland, 10 hours north of my parents in Newcastle, New South Wales. I hung up the phone and, with tears in my eyes, turned to my husband, Ross. "Pack the car. We're going to Newcastle."

"What? Now?"

"Pack the car."

We drove through the night, pulling up at dad's house just as the sun was rising. As he opened the door, we were greeted by a surprised look. He could barely utter a word, before the emotion began pouring from his eyes. We headed to the hospital, only for mum's equally startled face to soon be wet with tears too. Mum never cried. I knew this wasn't good.

We stayed until Sunday night but had to return ready for work on Monday. As we headed up the highway, emotionally exhausted, I let everything out. "I don't want a phone call," I sobbed. "This is too much. I'm sick of it. We're moving back to Newcastle."

It was a pivotal weekend and one that would change the course of my future. Things weren't going that well anyway in Brisbane, so we knew now was a good time to make a shift. Looking through the newspaper, there was an advertisement for a national franchise manager with an education centre. I had no idea what that was. I didn't know anything about franchising. I didn't know anything about what a national franchise manager did. And I knew nothing about tutoring organisations. However,

I had a teaching degree, I was good with people, and I knew I was organised. I figured that might be enough to get me the job.

I applied for the job through a recruitment company, nearly coming to blows with the recruiter in the process. I'm not going to get myself put forward here now, I thought. Surprisingly, he did. He put me forward.

I met with the founders, Kip and Dug (short for Dagnija in Latvian) McGrath from Kip McGrath Education Centres, who were impressed enough during the interview to offer me $40,000 a year. It was about $7000 less than I was on in Brisbane and sounded like a crummy job.

But I took the job. In August 2000, we packed up our home in Brisbane and moved in with my parents for a while in Newcastle until we could get our own place. By December, I still wasn't sold on this job being a long-term gig.

Kip somehow picked up on my internal monologue. He called me into his office.

"I really like the work you're doing," he said. "You can make a decision."

Can't everybody, I thought.

"So, here's a $5000 pay rise."

I decided that would keep me there for a few more months. After working in government jobs, I'd become used to pay rises never happening.

Another six months passed, and I got called in again. "I've got a proposition for you. I know you're really ambitious." I'd always wanted to be a manager, but by this stage I was pretty much a glorified admin person putting systems in place to keep everything together.

I put the systems in place not for any other reason than to make my own life easier. Instead of someone dumping a pile of contracts on the floor and saying, "they're due, figure it out", I systematically went through each and created a spreadsheet. It wasn't anything special – just the basic information and when it was due next. None of it was rocket science.

So here I was, 37 years of age and wanting to learn, grow and become a manager. I didn't have any staff to manage, yet I was coordinating everybody.

"I really like what you're doing here, and I really want you to stay," Kip said. "I'll give you three years of management training, if you'll give me five years of service. You'll go from $45,000 to $100,000 over the next three years. We'll set some milestones for you to reach." Within the first six months, he wanted me to learn to say no to the franchisees, which I'd struggled with.

During the six months, he would give me management training. I'd sit in his office, he'd train me or, if I made a mistake, I'd get reprimanded and trained on that.

I remember one time when a franchisee from Tasmania was selling her franchise. The training fee for the incoming franchisees had recently increased. On a Friday at 4.45pm, she rang to say she didn't want to pay the increased fee. "It's not for me to pay that for the incoming franchisee." Of course, it didn't have to come out of her pocket. She could on charge that to the new franchisee.

I sighed, told her I'd find out what we could do and toddled off to Kip's office. I sat directly in front of him and asked him: "what should I tell her?" He looked at me. "Shirley, it's almost 5pm on a Friday afternoon. You know the answer to this question. Why are we having this conversation? Learn to say no."

He was right. I dragged myself back to the phone. "Well, I know this isn't what you want to hear," I began, "but that's the cost and you can pass it on. But you are responsible for paying us."

From then on, I trusted myself to say no and never went back into his office to ask again. Every six months, we would have a series of milestones. At the end of that six months, I'd have mastered a new skill.

Ross looked at me one day. "It's like you put on a new jacket at the beginning of the six months. It's as uncomfortable as hell. And then after a couple of months, you get it and loosen up in the jacket. It starts to feel good. And then, guess what? That jacket comes off and the process starts again with a new uncomfortable jacket."

After wearing so many jackets, I reached a point where I was basically running the place. Kip and his son Storm did the selling, wife Dug was responsible for curriculum, and I was now the most senior executive officer that wasn't a family member. All this in just three and half years, not to mention more than doubling my salary. I have to say, working in a private enterprise suited me.

There is no way this could have happened in my government jobs. What started out as "a crummy job", turned out to be one of the best experiences I've had. I was there for six years, and I still quote Kip's teachings to this day.

If you've just put on a new lieutenant's jacket and it's feeling all too uncomfortable, know you're not alone. I've helped hundreds of lieutenants gain a wardrobe full of comfortable jackets much sooner than they expected. With this book, you can too.

# Chapter 2
# The Science of Business Freedom

Before we get into the role of the Second-In-Command, and why yours is the most important role in the organisation, it's important to look at what we mean by The Science of Business Freedom and how this affects you and your boss. In most cases, entrepreneurs and business owners go into business expecting to have a life they love. They dream about having time and money freedom, yet frequently find themselves working for the hardest boss they've ever had. They have little time and little freedom, and some have little money. Michael Gerber, author of *The E-Myth*, highlights this phenomenon.

According to Gerber, and my experience working with thousands of small business owners, business owners start out in the role of technicians. They are good at what they do and are generally good at sales and marketing. Before long the business grows, and they find they need help. They can't keep up with orders and there are too many operational tasks to take care of. In their desperation they usually hire family members who are happy to help, but not necessarily the most skilled or experienced people for the roles.

The business owner now finds himself responsible for recruiting and training people, and leading and managing them. This is often with little formal training in leadership or management, and all while having to make the products or deliver the services. The more people he employs, the more time it takes and the more stressed he feels. Eventually, he starts to understand the role of business owner, which according to Gerber, is to work ON rather than IN the business. Working ON the business means looking at the bigger picture. It's about creating the vision and strategy to get there. It's keeping abreast of technology and the competition and finding innovative ways to do things. Think of it this way, the president or CEO of any bank is responsible for consistently delivering value to its shareholders. His time and energy are devoted to working ON the business. He is not the technician. He is not the cashier or loan assessor. Until the business owner understands and accepts the role of business owner and recruits and empowers an efficient Second-In-Command, there is no way he can enjoy time and money freedom or the lifestyle of his dreams.

When you analyse what is happening, it's no surprise the Bank of America (2015) reported that, on average, 85% of small business owners work more than 40 hours each week. It also shared that 30% worked 60+ hours, and 67% of small business owners are more likely to delay or reduce their own compensation to make ends meet. Clearly, this is not business freedom. To see where you or your boss sit on the Time and Money Freedom Matrix, go to https://shirleydalton.com/2IC.

When I was working with Kip, I travelled around Australia providing refresher training to the franchisees. After a session in Melbourne one day, I received a card from one of the franchisees who thanked me for the training and mentioned how I was a loyal lieutenant to Kip. This is what you're striving to be. To achieve business freedom, the boss needs a loyal lieutenant, a Second-In-Command. Someone who loves leading and managing people, is detail oriented and organised and gets stuff done. In Chapter 3, you'll learn 15 reasons why your role is the most important in the organisation.

To achieve time and money freedom, you first need a vision for where the business is going and the reason it exists. That's the CEO's job (or as we now say, the CVO's job – Chief Vision Officer, as taught by Simon Sinek).

Once you know where the business is headed and why, you need the following things to have a successful business which can lead to time and money freedom:

1. Efficient, effective and consistent business processes.

2. The right people employed in the right roles.

3. A clear understanding of the purpose for each role, and the knowledge, experience, skills, attitude and qualifications (KESAQ) required for each role.

4. Induction and training programs for your people.

5. Key Performance and Key Behaviour indicators to ensure company standards are consistently met and delivered.

6. Leaders with good leadership and communication skills.

7. Well documented or recorded policies and procedures.

In short, you need to focus on three areas: your people, processes and possibilities.

Business freedom is attainable. We call it the Science of Business Freedom because it is a science. You can learn and develop the skills and processes you need.

Go to [https://shirleydalton.com/2IC](https://shirleydalton.com/2IC) to learn more about the Blueprint for Business Freedom.

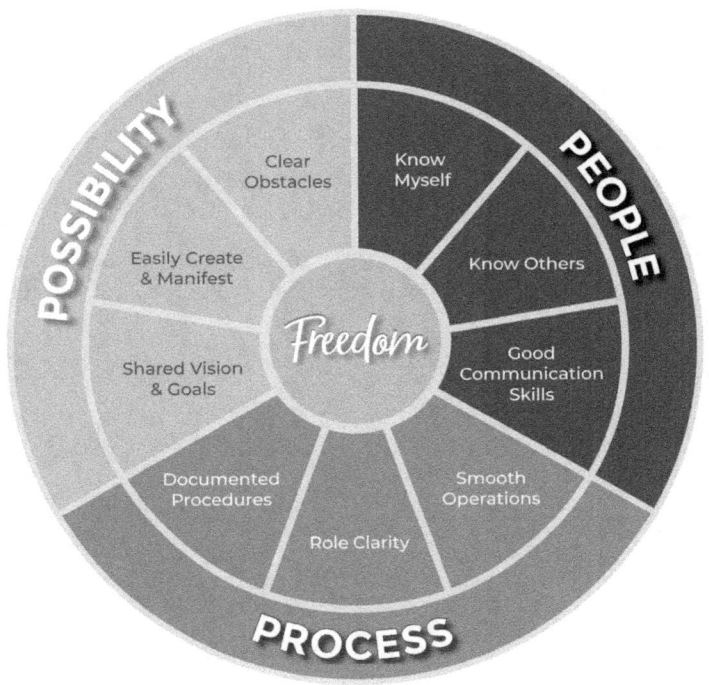

If you want more time, money, freedom and authority, you need to convince your boss she too can have more time, money and freedom. And the way for her to achieve that, is to empower you to do what you do best and that is, run the company.

The remainder of this book is dedicated to showing you how.

# Chapter 3
# Why You Are So Needed and So Valuable

If you're reading this book, I assume you are the official or unofficial go-to-person in your organisation. You are formally or informally "The Second-In-Command", the 2IC.

You care about the organisation, your boss and your team.

You have passion, drive and a motivation to succeed.

You enjoy working and love achieving results.

You love people, even though they can frustrate you at times. It's because of you the team achieves as much as it does.

Your boss needs you and, whether he will admit it openly or not, he can't do without you. So, let's look at the 15 most important things the boss wants and how you – the Second-In-Command and the one who runs the organisation – can deliver, every single time.

## 1.     Someone To Rely On

The boss wants someone she can rely on to get things done. The boss sees the end goal but has no patience or eye for detail to get there. She needs to know that you, the loyal lieutenant, is there for the team, the customers and the business.

I really got to understand this one morning when I couldn't open the door to my garage to drive to work on time. This day was an important one. The boss and I were training new franchisees and it was my job to be at work early to prepare for the day. I wasn't able to let my boss know I would be late. When I eventually arrived at work, he came rushing out to greet me.

"Are you alright?" he asked. "You're always here on time and you know how important today is. I was very concerned something had happened to you."

Having someone they can rely on gives them peace of mind and frees them up to do what they do best. When was the last time you took time off? A boss, too, deserves more time, money and freedom.

## 2. Sounding Board And Teacher

Your boss wants a sounding board; someone who can listen and isn't afraid to ask the hard questions or give feedback when required. It doesn't hurt if they're able to teach the boss a thing or two as well.

One of my strengths is communication. I have spent years learning and refining my skills. I cringe when I hear people use "You Statements" instead of "I Messages".

"What's a 'You Statement'?" you might ask.

A "You Statement" is a statement that starts with "You" and is usually followed by a description of what the person did or didn't do. It's assigning blame to others, and it usually provokes a defensive response. For example, "You didn't phone when you said you would." "You didn't finish the job. You're so lazy." It's much better to use an "I Message", where you describe things from your point of view. It lands better for the other person. Because you are telling them how it is for you, they can't dispute it. It always starts with "I", not "You". For example, "I was expecting to speak with you at 4pm" or "I'm disappointed the job wasn't finished. I had to stay back an extra two hours to get it done."

The reason I'm telling you this is that I taught many bosses how to communicate using "I Messages". They would draft a letter and then call me in to show me how they had incorporated "I Messages". They were proud of how diplomatic and tactful their communication had become, compared to when I first started working with them.

Go to https://shirleydalton.com/2IC to learn more about the four types of "I Messages" and how to construct them.

There are many things you can teach your boss. Being Second-In-Command doesn't mean your boss knows everything.

## 3. Defining Results

Your boss wants to define and outline specific objectives or goals to achieve. He won't necessarily know how to get there nor be the best person to provide "how to" instructions. He wants you to see the vision and then reverse engineer to come up with a plan to get the result. It's your job to come up with the step-by-step instructions, systems, and processes for the team to follow.

One of my clients imports kitchens from China and sells them to customers who want to install them themselves. He wanted to know the status of each customer's order. He wanted to be able to look at something and see the status of the orders at a glance. He couldn't work out the system and so he called me in. It was my job, together with the administration, design and sales teams, to design a system that could deliver the end result. At the end of the project he had what he wanted. We were able to show him the status electronically and on a whiteboard.

He was very happy. In fact, when I visited him a few months after the project, he said, "Hear that?" "Hear what?" I asked. "The business", he replied, "It just hums. There is no chaos or confusion. It even sounds good." That made me happy.

Being able to problem solve and deliver solutions increases your value tenfold and more.

## 4. Done Yesterday

The boss wants it done yesterday because she's busy selling new products today. This places enormous pressure on your team, and yet you can handle it. You must be able to prioritise, delegate and manage the resources you have, if you're going to meet the deadlines and cope with the lightning-fast pace.

You also need the ability and courage to negotiate deadlines and priorities. One question I teach my clients and staff to ask their boss is, "What is your priority?" For example, when asked to complete an urgent job when you have a number of other competing priorities, you might say, "I can certainly get that done for you by <insert required time frame>. To do that though will mean I need to re-organise some of the tasks I am currently working on. Could you please let me know your priorities for these tasks <list the tasks and how long you expect it will take to complete them>?" Asking this question does two things:

- It alerts the boss to how much work people have
- It gives the boss the authority and responsibility to make the call for the priorities.

## 5. Lead And Manage The Team

The boss wants you to manage the team, mediate any upsets and delegate to the team. The boss doesn't want the stress of supervising the team. That's your job. But he will notice if the team is failing.

Being on time was important to one of my bosses. Unfortunately for me and one of my team members Max, he would often follow Max in to work after the 9am start time. Max's office was on a level below mine, so I wasn't aware he was late until my boss called me on the phone from his office.

"Shirley, I just followed Max into the office, again."

"Argh! Thank you. I'll take care of it."

You know that feeling when you really wish you didn't have to hold your team accountable and yet you do. You step up and do what's required. You have that conversation. In this case, I requested Max come to my office. I described the situation and asked for his commitment to arrive at work on time. The conversation went something like this:

"Max, Mr Jones informed me he followed you into work just now. Could I confirm please that you have just arrived or is it possible you were here earlier and had left the building and are now returning?"

"No, I just arrived."

"This is really awkward for me. I am your supervisor, and I was not aware that on a number of occasions Mr Jones has followed you into work, after the start time. Are there any extenuating circumstances I am not aware of that are causing you to arrive after start time?"

"No, I just find it difficult to get up in the morning and sometimes I have to drop the kids off at school."

"Dropping the kids makes you late?"

"No, not really, I can drop them before school starts. They have before and after school care."

"Max, it's a condition of your employment that you start on time. I really don't want to have this conversation again and I certainly don't want Mr Jones calling me and informing me he's followed you in. You say the school has before and after care for kids. Is this something you could look into, to help you get to work on time?"

"Yeah. I'll look into it."

"Okay, thank you, I appreciate that. When do you think you'll be able to do that and let me know?"

"I can ask this afternoon when I pick the kids up and let you know tomorrow."

"Great, thank you and please be on time tomorrow."

"Yeah, I will."

Leading and managing the team and having these conversations can be uncomfortable, which is why we include communication training skills such as "I Messages", active listening and conflict resolution skills in our Leading Yourself and Leading Others experience.

It's also a part of individual executive coaching sessions.

These skills can be learned and, when implemented, you'll find your relationships improve and your need to have confronting conversations will decrease.

## 6. Happy Customers

The boss wants to know the customers are being looked after and are happy. She loves to hear what a great decision she made to employ you. She will beam with pride when customers share their praise for you and your team.

The director of property management for one of my real estate clients had to fill in and complete routine property inspections whilst he found a replacement for the property officer, who had been promoted within the organisation. During one inspection, the tenants asked about the property officer. "Where is Norma?" they asked. "How come Norma isn't doing the inspection?" The director informed them Norma had been promoted and they were in the process of replacing her. "That's wonderful news," replied the tenant. "She is a great property officer and we really liked her. She was so organised and on top of everything. Nothing was a problem." A very happy boss agreed, "She was indeed a rare find, and we're very lucky to have her."

## 7. Make Decisions And Take Responsibility

It was just after lunch and my boss called me into his office.

As I stood in the doorway with nothing in my hands, he looked at me quite seriously and said,

"Shirley, I want you to lose that piece of paper."

I was perplexed. I didn't have a piece of paper and I said so.

"I'm talking about the one that you cover your butt with," he continued.

"You're not in the government now. I want you to make decisions and take responsibility. If you make a wrong decision, simply make another one. Stop wasting time covering your butt with emails and notes."

It was a confronting yet true observation and, oddly, it allowed me to give myself permission to accept the responsibility I had been given and, indeed, make more decisions.

## 8.   Say "No"

This was perhaps one of my biggest, longest and hardest lessons. There were so many occasions when I had the opportunity to say "No" and I didn't have the courage. What I learned was it was far easier to take the pain and say "No" rather than stretch it out when the outcome was going to be the same.

As mentioned, in the franchise organisation I shouldn't have had to ask whether we could reduce the training fee for the outgoing franchisee. I should have had the courage to stand by the company policy and say "No".

As the Second-In-Command, there will be many times when your courage is tested. It's far better for all concerned if you can say "No" sooner rather than later.

## 9. Improve The Business

Your boss wants you to be thinking about improving his business. One day, Kip stopped at my office door and said, "Shirley, if I walk past your office and I see you with your back to the door staring out the window, I'll be really happy." I had no idea what he was referring to, so I replied with "Okay, I'll bite. What do you mean?" He replied, "If I see you staring out the window, I'll know you are thinking about my business and how you can improve it." And with that he walked off.

It's okay to sit and think. In fact, that's another lesson I learned, that of "Thinking Time". Thinking Time is giving yourself the time to sit and think on a consistent basis. This helps train your mind to solve problems. My Thinking Time was on Mondays at 8am before the rest of the team started work. I would take myself upstairs to the boardroom and sit with a blank piece of paper and a cup of tea. Some mornings I would have a question and the answers would come easily. On other days, I would sit and look at the paper and nothing would come. It's important to schedule Thinking Time and to persist. Eventually, your problem-solving brain will become accustomed to solving problems and you won't have to schedule the time. If you're not allowing yourself Thinking Time, I highly recommend you schedule at least an hour a week to simply sit and think.

One other important point – it's best to do your thinking in the same place each week.

Remember to take a pen and some paper to record your solutions.

## 10. Be Efficient And Effective

A consulting client of mine told me how impressed he was with Georgia, one of his team members. "Oh, she's fabulous, such a great find. She's here before everyone in the morning and often stays back till 7pm, when all the others leave at 5pm. I don't think I've employed anyone as dedicated as Georgia."

I paid particular attention to Georgia as I was working with the team on their operations. I found Georgia to be the opposite to what the boss thought. The real reason she started early and finished late wasn't because she was efficient. In fact, it was quite the opposite; she was totally inefficient and ineffective during the day. She gossiped and stopped others from working. She got involved in others' tasks instead of completing her own. If she had paid attention to her own work, she could have saved herself those additional hours at work. Your boss wants you to be efficient and not have to work after hours, and she wants you to ensure the team does so as well.

## 11. Team Respect

The boss wants the team to respect you. When I first started supervising people, I turned to a previous boss of mine who gave me great advice. "The first rule of management; it's not a popularity contest. You can be friendly; you can't be their friend." I learned that being respected was far more important and productive than being a friend. As another of my clients says, "I don't socialise with the staff because it's too awkward if I go to their birthday party on Saturday and have to sack them on Monday."

That's not to say I didn't learn a few lessons along the way. When I was given supervision of my first team, four women, one of the tasks was performance reviews. I told the boss, "I'm going to go over the road and have a cup of coffee with the ladies when I do their performance reviews." He looked at me sternly. "Yeah, you can do that. But how's their coffee going to taste when you have to fail them one day?" Eventually, I did have to fail one of my team, and I was grateful to be in the office.

I also learned not to do reviews on a Wednesday, after having to deal with a grumpy team member for the rest of the week. After that, reviews were always done on a Friday afternoon, so they had the weekend to get over it if they happened to fail (thankfully not many did).

## 12. Train The Team

Your boss wants you to train the team. Training starts with your on boarding and induction process. The clearer you are at the beginning, the fewer issues you'll have along the way. Keep in mind your induction needs to be consistent, so everyone receives the same information and has the same expectations.

Checklists can be extremely useful. Having a checklist also means someone else can be trained to complete the inductions and still ensure consistency.

I often assist my clients with recruitment and, when I interview candidates, I always ask them how they like to learn. This saves the employer a lot of time and energy. If someone wants to read procedures, give them procedures. If others want to be shown how, give them demonstrations and teach them. Still, others prefer to figure it out for themselves and ask questions. It is important to know the learning styles of your people. Whether visual, auditory or kinaesthetic, you'll save yourself time and angst if you train them in the way they learn best.

Go to [https://shirleydalton.com/2IC](https://shirleydalton.com/2IC) for samples of Induction Checklists and three different ways to teach the same topic.

## 13. Develop Systems And Processes, And Delegate To The Team

As the Second-In-Command, you'll get to work on more interesting and strategic projects when you can take what you know, systemise it and delegate it to other team members. For example, one of my jobs was to send birthday cards to our customers. I prided myself on having the card arrive on their birthday or as close to it if it was a weekend. I knew how many days in advance I needed to post the cards. Unless I shared this knowledge, I was always going to be responsible for the cards. I simply created a list of the customer birthdays for each month and recorded the number of days to send the card before the birthday. I was then able to delegate this job, which freed up my time to work on more interesting and higher-level projects.

Another area to look for improvements is customer complaints. When I first joined one organisation, I received many complaints about parcels being delivered to the wrong address. After talking with the dispatch manager, I found the courier company we used didn't deliver to post office boxes, only premises. I asked the customers for their preference for parcel deliveries and the problem was solved. What complaints are you receiving? These present great opportunities to develop systems and processes to fix the issues, save the team and promote yourself to your boss.

## 14. Awareness of Company Finances

You're not expected to be the chief financial officer (CFO) or the accounts manager. But you do need to know when the customers are falling behind and be able to have that conversation with them. It's also a good idea if you are aware of the profitability of the company overall and can monitor your expenditure and manage your resources.

When I started my own business and had to pay for stationery, I soon learned not to waste resources. Your boss will certainly appreciate it. Here's a story that still brings tears to my eyes.

I employed a junior and it was her first administrative role. I asked her to print 150 flyers in colour. I should have instructed her to test one first. Instead, I walked past her desk and there were 300 pages of coloured flyers. Each page was supposed to be printed with a red border. The border had not been properly formatted and printed over two pages, giving us 300 coloured pages that couldn't be used for anything other than scrap paper.

Your value will increase tremendously if you demonstrate your awareness of company finances and use your resources efficiently.

## 15. Keep Good Records

Finally, you must have good records and be able to manage company documents. If the boss is out selling things that don't exist and you're in charge of managing the team and operations, you need to be able to access important documents at a minute's notice. Good record keeping and filing are about ease of retrieval.

When the company I worked for listed on the Australian Stock Exchange, we had to prove every statement we made about the company in the prospectus. The auditor and the legal teams all came to me when they needed to check their facts. Why? Because I was the one who knew exactly where everything was. This is your job and I know you're great at this. In fact, your team and almost everyone in the organisation knows it and counts on you to be able to source or reference information when needed.

## What The Boss Wants Is You

Yours in the most important role in the company. You are the most important person in the organisation.

You are the glue that keeps it stuck together. Without you, the company would fall apart.

Remember, if you want more time, money, freedom and authority, you need to convince your boss she too can have more time, money and freedom.

The way to achieve that is to empower you to do what you do best and that is, run the company operations.

Your role is the sweet spot holding it all together between the boss, the people and the operations. You are the linchpin for the company's people, processes and possibilities.

Now that you get your value, it's time to commit to being the company champion and implement The 5 Steps To Business Freedom, so you can be handsomely rewarded and recognised for your results.

In the coming chapters, I will take you through four of those five steps. The additional one is to step up and make the decision to be the leader.

# SECTION 2

# 4 SIMPLE STEPS TO BUSINESS FREEDOM

## Chapter 4
## Step 1: Map Your Processes

Known as Mapping Your Processes or Charting the Customer Experience, the first and most important step is to identify "**Who** does **What** and **When** and **Why**?" In other words, we create a workflow by starting with WHAT HAPPENS, by WHOM, WHEN and HOW.

Asking these questions enables you to create what we call a Workflow Diagram or Flow Chart. The Workflow Diagram can then be used as the basis for the following three steps.

The question of **"Who"** refers to the roles that are responsible for the tasks. Please don't refer to individuals when you do this because individuals come and go, as in "That's Joe's job". This is a really important point. "Who" always relates to a role title or position. For example, receptionist or sales representative. Every company has their own system for job titles, which is why it's important to write down the role titles used in your business and not that of other businesses.

The **"What"** refers to the task to be completed. It is a brief description, generally no more than a few words.

**"When"** refers to the order the tasks are completed. For example, step 1 comes before step 2, before step 3, etc.

Asking **"Why"** enables you to question why you do what you do and to identify gaps and areas for improvement. For example, you may find as you go through the workflow that it's no longer necessary to post invoices to customers because your accounting software enables you to email the invoices directly to them. The task is still the same in that you invoice customers. However, the way you do it may change because of these discussions.

Before you start, you'll need to decide what you're going to document. You can start with one section of your business; this could be the area that is causing the most problems. It could be accounts receivable or the area where you can make the most gains. Or you can look to document the entire company processes from end-to-end to deliver your product or service.

# Gather The Information

To create your Workflow Diagram, you'll need to first gather the information from your team members. In my role as a consultant, I've found the hardest thing for people to do is to unpack what they know. There is a huge difference between doing a task and teaching others how to do the task.

There are three ways you can gather the information.

## *Method 1*

You can talk to your workers individually and find out what they do, how they do it and why they do it that way. For example, when I first started my consulting business, I made the mistake of assuming two ladies who shared a job would do it the same way. The job involved entering data for new customers. One lady liked to complete all 12 steps for each customer before moving onto the next. The other preferred to batch the steps and do step 1 for all new customers before moving on to steps 2 and 3 etc. Either method was correct. What couldn't be changed were the 12 steps and the information required. When gathering information, be sure to identify the critical steps and information required. It's always better to speak with workers than to ask them to complete a template, especially when they are explaining the steps they take. Our neurology is such that we don't think and talk in a linear logical fashion. Often you will find the worker will miss a step or two as they describe how they complete tasks. It's important to remain alert, so you can notice if the steps are incomplete.

## *Method 2*

Facilitate a team meeting to determine the workflow. Invite the team to discuss who does what, when and why, and capture this information on a whiteboard or specialist software program so everyone can see.

## *Method 3*

Hybrid. Talk to workers individually, document the workflow based on what you learn. Then invite the team to meet and go through the workflow to make sure:

- It is correct
- The team understands everyone's roles and effectively engages with the process.

## Creating the Workflow Diagram

If you're going to use a whiteboard or flip chart paper, you'll need a different coloured marker or Post-It Note for each role. Or you may prefer to create the chart using a specialist software program.

The Workflow Diagram consists of boxes joined by arrows pointing to the next task. A diamond shape is used to signify a decision that needs to be made and often branches off into two or more boxes. The boxes are used to identify and briefly describe the "What". The order of the boxes determines "When" the task

The Loyal Lieutenant

or process is to be completed. The colour of the box shows what role is responsible for the task. There are many ways to create a Workflow Diagram. To download samples of completed Workflow Diagrams for different industries, go to https://shirleydalton.com/2IC

Generally, I start at the top left-hand side of the whiteboard, flip chart or page in a software program such as Lucid Chart or Microsoft Visio. Choose any colour and draw a box to start the diagram.

**Advertising & Marketing**

We will use the example of mapping the customer experience, so we'll start with a box for Advertising and Marketing.

Colour the border of the box to denote the role, (not the person). Document the associated roles and colours in a separate Legend off to the side of the workflow. Note: only use colour on the border of the box while you create the workflow on the whiteboard or flip chart. You can fill the boxes with colour if you create the Workflow Diagram in a software program or if you need to include a different colour for a different role, because two roles can complete the task.

**Legend Example:**

Marketing Manager

Receptionist

Sales Representative

Draw an arrow from the Advertising and Marketing box horizontally to another box. Label it with a brief description of the "What". For example, "Initial Enquiry".

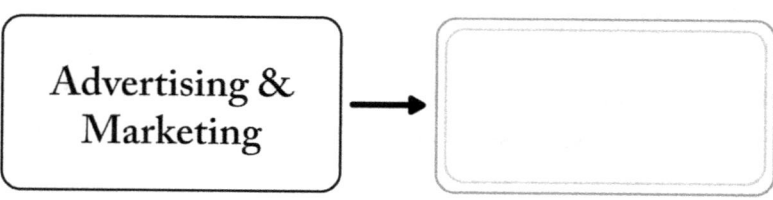

Colour the border of the box to represent the role that handles the Initial Enquiry. If there are multiple roles that can do this job, simply add multiple colours to the border of the box or colour the inside of the box with a different colour. For example, either your receptionist or sales representative may handle an Initial Enquiry from a customer (two separate border colours).

Ask yourself or your team what happens next.

What happens with your Initial Enquiry? Does it come via the phone, website, email, social media enquiry or in person?

Do you have a script and/or enquiry form for handling enquiries? If not, go to https://shirleydalton.com/2IC to download Sample Enquiry Forms.

What happens next after the Initial Enquiry? What role takes over from here?

The Loyal Lieutenant

Or is it the same role that handles the Initial Enquiry? Draw another box underneath the Initial Enquiry with a downward arrow joining the two boxes. In the example below, the sales representative meets the prospective customer onsite at their premises. What happens in your company?

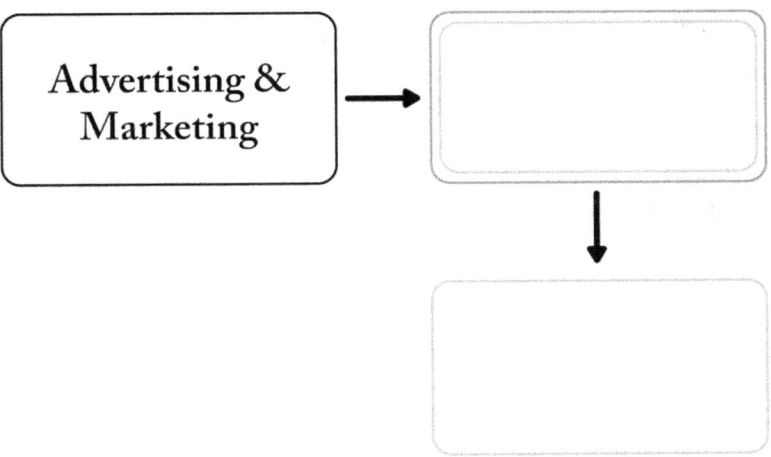

Continue adding boxes for the next task or group of tasks in the sequence. Document the "What" in an abbreviated form in the box. Colour the border of the box according to the role, and add to the Legend if needed.

Continue the process asking "What happens next? What role does that?"

You can go into as much or as little detail as you like with this process. Be mindful, that too much detail will prolong the process and could become overwhelming. Too few details will not provide enough information for people to know what to do.

Keep creating task boxes and joining them to the tasks before, after or to the side of each other with the arrows.

Use a diamond instead of a box to indicate when decisions must be made. For example, your sales representative may provide a proposal to a customer which will either be accepted or rejected. That's a decision that leads to two different sets of tasks – yes, leads to ordering materials and no, leads to follow-up activities.

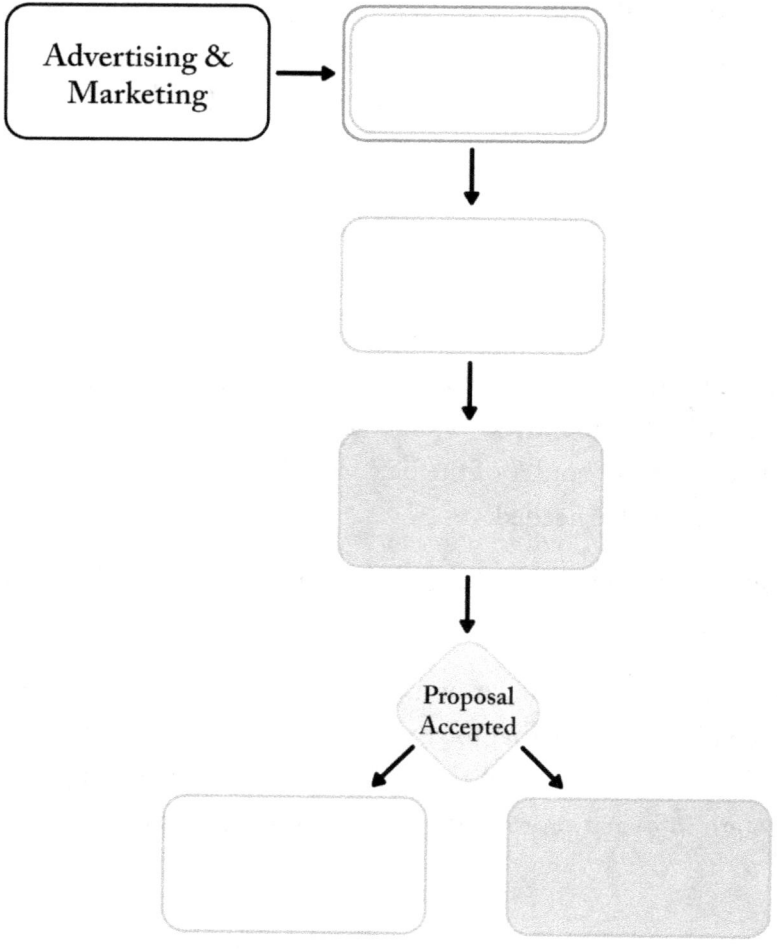

## Capturing Sub-Tasks

For many of your tasks there will be sub-tasks. It's not necessary to add boxes for every sub-task. These can be captured in a list next to the box on the Flow Chart or documented in a checklist that is referred to in the Flow Chart. For example, the task might be to order parts for a customer, which includes sub-tasks as shown below:

Check inventory

| Order Parts | • Complete order
• Submit order
• File order |

OR

| Order Parts | • Refer Order Checklist |

Depending on the size of your organisation or department being documented, you may find your Workflow Diagram becomes complex. You can use all the available space on your page or add extra pages. You can go across, up and down your page, but ensure you include arrows to show the direction of the processes.

**Assignment 1:**

1. Choose which method you will use to gather information (individual or team meeting). If you choose a team meeting, you will also need to choose how you will capture the data from the team. For example, whiteboard, flip chart or a software program.

2. Create your Workflow Diagram (go to https://shirleydalton.com/2IC to download sample Workflow Diagrams to compare).

3. When you have completed your first draft, ask your workers to review and provide feedback on the Workflow Diagram to ensure you have correctly captured Who (role) does What (the box), When (the sequence) and Why (identifies areas for improvement and helps team members understand why their co-workers insist on various procedures being followed. In essence, it promotes teamwork when the team can see how their work directly impacts their co-workers).

4. Edit your diagram as required.

5. Ensure all involved agree the diagram correctly represents Who does What and When, and that the team agrees to follow the processes from here on.

6. Create any forms or change and improve procedures resulting from the assignment.

7. Show your boss and explain the process you went through.

8. If the boss agrees, display the completed Workflow Diagram where workers can easily refer to it. This will also help you with training and accountability.

Remember:

EVERYTHING IS DRAFT UNTIL IT IS FINAL.

Don't get attached to your diagram. Not everyone has your skills and it's easier for others to edit, tweak and make comments than to start from scratch (that's your job).

EVERYTHING IS DRAFT UNTIL IT IS FINAL.

Please remember that and share it with your team, so they understand that you want their feedback to ensure correctness. This isn't about not saying something in case it hurts someone's feelings. Tell them you won't be offended if they suggest changes.

# Chapter 5
# Step 2: Your Organisation Structure

Now you know Who does What and When and Why, it's time to create your Organisation Chart. This outlines the roles your organisation needs to be able to complete all the tasks. It's why it was so important to capture roles in the Who of the workflow, and not individuals such as Joe or Bob.

Make a list of all the roles you coloured in your Workflow Diagram. You can get this by referring to your Legend. For example, marketing manager, receptionist, sales representative.

This will help you determine the key areas in your business. Generally, a business needs the following key business areas:

1. Advertising and Marketing
2. Sales
3. Finance
4. Administration
5. Production
6. Dispatch
7. Human Resources
8. Information Technology
9. Work Health & Safety, Environment & Quality Assurance

From this information you can create what is known as a Functional Organisation Chart because it shows the functions or roles that are required. (Go to https://shirleydalton.com/2IC for an example for real estate. Even if you're not in the real estate business, most people have either bought, sold or rented somewhere to live).

When you download the Organisation Chart for Real Estate, you'll find the managing director sits at the top, with his executive assistant reporting directly to him. The executive assistant appears as if she is out on her own.

Below the managing director is a line of boxes, similar to a football team, with a box for each of the business areas within the organisation:

1. Sales
2. Marketing
3. Administration
4. Accounts/Finance
5. Human Resources
6. Information Technology
7. Compliance
8. Health Safety and Environment
9. Property Management

Underneath sales, you will find the various divisions for selling real estate:

1. Residential Sales
2. Commercial Sales
3. Industrial Sales

Below marketing, you'll find a box for the marketing coordinator.

Below administration, a box for the administration officer.

Below finances, a box for the financial controller. Below that, a box for the sales and property management trust administrators and accounts assistant.

Human resources has a box for the human resources manager and, below that, a box for the human resources assistant.

Information technology includes an IT coordinator.

Compliance has a compliance officer.

Health safety and environment has a box for the HSE coordinator.

Lastly, property management has a manager, who has two rows of boxes below that. In other words, reporting upwards to the manager are boxes for property managers and property officers who report to the property managers.

Your Organisation Chart will be unique to your business. You may have boxes for roles that manufacture goods or run a warehouse. Your business may provide services rather than products, so you may need boxes for consultants or hair stylists and apprentices.

The detail of the chart is unique. What you will find though is most Organisation Charts are similar in format; they represent the owner or CEO or CVO at the top of the chart and then cascade according to the roles that report to each other.

Start with the CEO, managing director, president or whatever title you use in your company. Place this box in the middle top of your page or whiteboard. From there, create boxes for the

*The Loyal Lieutenant*

roles that report directly to the boss. There may be one or many. Remember, we're talking roles, not individual names. Enter the title for the role into the box.

Study each role (box) to determine whether they have any roles reporting to them. If so, use connecting lines and boxes to record the role titles. Keep adding boxes until all roles have been included on the chart. Check the roles against the Legend in your Workflow Diagram to make sure you haven't missed any.

You can now fill in details of worker names. You may find that some worker's names are included in several roles. That's perfectly OK. There is no rule that says each box must represent a different person. In fact, in small businesses, often the boss' name is in all the boxes when they first start the business.

You also have a choice whether to colour code the boxes for the roles or leave them the one colour. Either is acceptable.

One final point on using the Organisation Chart. You can document the roles as they are now, or you can use the chart as a visioning tool. If you use it this way, think about the roles you want to create for the future and add them to your chart. You can then define when you will fill the roles according to a time frame or perhaps an achieved revenue goal.

One CEO I consulted to was able to envision growing her company from 9 to 84 employees. So, we created her Organisation Chart based on 84 roles.

Another company director used the chart to set a goal to replace herself in various roles. She gave herself a time frame and an action plan to train a replacement, so she could move into a more strategic role within the company. She achieved her goal within six months. Within three years, she and her husband had replaced themselves entirely and went sailing in north Queensland in Australia for six months.

## Assignment 2

1. Follow the directions above and use your Workflow Diagram and Legend to create and document your Organisation Chart.
2. Invite your workers to review and provide feedback.
3. Edit your chart as required
4. Show your boss and describe the process you used
5. If your boss agrees, finalise your chart and display.
6. You can use this chart to identify where you have a need for recruitment, or perhaps you are doubling up with people doing the same role. You can also use it to envision where you might want the company to be in the future.

# Chapter 6
# Step 3: Role Clarity

Your people want to come to work to succeed in their roles. They want to know what they have to do and to what standard to succeed. If they are not succeeding, it is because they:

1. Don't know what to do
2. Don't know how to do it
3. Don't have the resources to do it
4. Don't want to do it.

Here's a mantra I learned from Kip McGrath a long time ago. It will help you determine whether it's a system problem or a people problem.

*"If staff don't give you what you want, either you didn't give good instructions, or they are incompetent. And if they are incompetent, is it because they are unable or unwilling? And if unable, do they need more training?"*

The best way to ensure success is to be clear about the role; the reason it exists or why it is important. We call this Key Performance Indicators (KPIs). The behaviours or tasks required, and to what standard, are known as Key Behaviour Indicators (KBIs). KPIs and KBIs are superior to job descriptions because a job description is often used to attract potential employees and can be vague around the standard to which the tasks need to be performed. For example, a job description might use language such as "responsible for processing company orders". A Key Behaviour Indicator would be more specific. For example, "Process orders within 24 hours of receipt of order. Orders to be complete and correct."

Now you have identified the roles you need in your organisation, you can create KPIs and KBIs for each role using the following formula.

## Key Performance Indicators (KPIs)

You can choose whether you want to include the role's contribution to company profitability. If so, document how.

An example for a sales role might be something like, "The majority of the company revenue is achieved through generating sales. The sales representative is responsible for identifying potential new customers, developing relationships, converting leads to sales, and maintaining and growing the existing customer base."

Whether you include contribution to company profitability or not, you must identify the top 3-5 outcomes for the position and include them for the Key Performance Indicators. This is because the outcomes dictate the behaviours or tasks that need to be done to achieve the outcomes. For example, answer the questions "Why does the position exist?" and "What is the bottom line for this role?"

In the role of national franchise manager, I was responsible for ensuring the franchisees continued to stay with the organisation. That was the bottom line or the overall outcome for the role. Keep them happy, keep them with us and keep them paying their franchise fees. This is what is known as a Key Performance Indicator. Often, Key Performance Indicators are the only measures companies use to determine whether employees are succeeding in their roles.

It is much more valuable to use both Key Performance Indicators and Key Behaviour Indicators.

## Key Behaviour Indicators (KBIs)

Key Behaviour Indicators describe the tasks or behaviours and the standard to which they need to be completed to succeed in the role.

Using the national franchise manager example, the outcome (KPI) was to retain happy franchisees.

Tasks or behaviours I completed to achieve this outcome included:

1. Calling and speaking to every franchisee at least four times per year.
2. Publishing an interesting newsletter on the 26th of the month.
3. Renewing franchise contracts before the expiry date.

In the example, it was easy to measure whether the national franchise manager called franchisees at least four times per year. I recorded the dates I called and spoke with the franchisees, and my boss could ask to see the spreadsheet at any time. He didn't need to micromanage me by asking daily whether I had made my calls. He could see the results in the spreadsheet. I had either made the calls or not made the calls. I'm not in favour of giving scores or making judgements other than asking, "Did the employee do it to the required standard or not?"

This makes it easy for you when you conduct your performance reviews. The tasks were either completed to standard or not. If not, look to the system first to see if there are extenuating circumstances. If not, look to your instructions or degree to which you have trained your employee. If you have trained them, given good instructions and there are no extenuating circumstances, it could be a case of the employee being unwilling. If so, you will need your communication skills to confront the performance.

Keep this in mind when you create your Key Behaviour Indicators. You are describing the tasks or behaviours that need to be performed to what standard. This ensures the measures are objective and not subjective when it comes time for performance reviews.

For example, one form of standard to measure could be a time frame. "Orders are correctly entered into the system within 24 hours of receipt."

Taking the time to clearly document each role in this way helps your workers to succeed in their work and enables you to go home feeling satisfied your workers are doing what they are meant to be doing to the correct standard.

## How To Document KBIs

1. Write a list of all the tasks needed to fulfil the outcomes or ask the worker what he or she does. For example, handle customer enquiries, process orders, receive payment, run sales reports, file reports.

2. Review the list and group like tasks together under a category heading. It might include Customer Service, Record Keeping etc.

3. Determine the standard for each task. Use something that is measurable in terms of time, quality, quantity, appearance etc. so the worker and supervisor can evaluate if the tasks are completed to standard. You can also ask the worker how they would know if this job or task was done correctly.

(Go to https://shirleydalton.com/2IC to download the template for creating KPIs and KBIs and to see samples for a real estate sales representative, property officer and sales representative selling commercial carpet.)

Because we have the standard for the work to be completed, we are only concerned with whether the worker does or does not complete the tasks to the required standard.

If so, congratulate the worker and apply any bonuses or rewards.

If not, investigate the reason. Is it a system problem, like "Enter orders correctly within 24 hours"? Perhaps there are too many orders to be physically processed within 24 hours, so you have a choice to extend the time to 48 hours or provide additional resources to meet the 24-hour standard.

If it's not a system problem but a worker issue, ask yourself whether it is because they are unable or unwilling. If unable, do they need more training? If unwilling, discipline may be required.

**Performance Reviews**

Having documented KPIs and KBIs makes it easy to conduct performance reviews for your workers.

I conduct performance reviews every quarter. The week the reviews are due, I notice the team reviewing their KPIs and KBIs to make sure they are doing what is expected of them.

When we have our formal meeting, it's as easy as going through each KBI and generally checking off that the worker has achieved the required standard for each. There are no surprises, and the worker does not have to be concerned about whether the boss is in a good mood or not. The process is 100% objective.

## Assignment 3

Follow the steps above to create KPIs and KBIs for one role in your organisation.

1. Write a list of all the tasks needed to fulfil the outcomes or ask the worker what he or she does.

2. Review the list and group like tasks together under a category heading. Use the template you downloaded to document your KPIs and KBIs.

3. Check the format against the samples you downloaded.

4. Determine the standard for each task. For example, something that is measurable in terms of time, quality, quantity, appearance etc, so the worker and supervisor can evaluate if the tasks are completed to standard.

5. Ask the worker to review and provide feedback on what you have documented.

6. Discuss and negotiate the standards or measures of success, as well as the tasks or behaviours you and the worker think belong to that role.

7. Edit the document as required.

8. Request the worker sign to say they agree with the KPIs and KBIs for their role. This is important because your KPIs and KBIs now form the basis for your performance reviews.

9. Give a copy to the worker.

10. Provide a copy to human resources for the worker's file.

11. Show your boss and explain the process. Then seek approval to create KPIs and KBIs for all roles within the organisation.

12. Continue to create KPIs and KBIs for the remaining roles. Repeat the process above.

# Chapter 7

# Step 4: Scale and Grow (Procedures – the How)

Step 4 is one of the most important steps to streamlining your business and getting back your time. This is critical if your workers are going to perform to the standards you require. Remember, your people want to succeed in their roles. Having documented procedures will help them do this.

You don't have to write a novel for every procedure.

As long as the steps are clear, your procedures can include written:

- Checklists
- Templates
- Workflow Diagrams
- Step-by-step instructions
- Drawings

They can also be recorded in other mediums, such as videos, podcasts or screen captures. There are numerous ways to document your procedures. The main thing to remember is people need to know what to DO.

Use verbs – doing words. For example, "Enter name, address and phone number; Call client using the telephone script."

Be clear about exactly what it is they must do. Use a step-by-step method where you can. Use simple language and keep it brief. And finally, make the procedures easy to find and use. There is no point having a big folder sitting on a desk gathering dust.

The procedures need to be user-friendly. Go to https://shirleydalton.com/2IC to download a template for writing procedures.

Your Workflow Diagram can be used to give you the Table of Contents for all the procedures you need to document and train your staff. Simply look at all the boxes in your Workflow

Diagram and list the tasks represented by each box. For example, Initial Enquiry, Order Parts, Conduct Onsite Visit, Prepare Proposal. This list is your Table of Contents because your workers need to know how to do the tasks to what standard for every box (task and sub-tasks).

You can group all the tasks that belong to each role together. This will help you to sort your procedures manual according to roles.

For example, you might have the following sections in your manual:

1. Advertising and Marketing
2. Sales
3. Production
4. Accounts Receivable
5. Accounts Payable
6. Dispatch of Goods

Every section will include the various procedures for all the tasks that fit that section or category. For example, Advertising and Marketing could include the following procedures:

1. Facebook Advertising
2. LinkedIn Advertising
3. Attending Networking Functions

Initially, it will be a big job to document all your procedures. However, having the Workflow Diagram at least gives you the Table of Contents for the procedures.

Use your list as a checklist and check them off once completed.

**Assignment 4**

1. Choose three procedures to document. To gain confidence, choose procedures that are:

    - Simple

    - Clear in how the task must be performed

    - Something the team are doing inconsistently or that needs to be completed consistently

2. Assume a beginner's mindset. Pretend you don't know anything about the task. List all the things that need to be done to complete the task – in order, i.e. step 1, step 2, step 3, etc.

3. Write your procedure starting with a verb for each step. A verb is a doing word. People want to know what they have to do.

4. Review the procedure with the workers who are responsible for the task to ensure all steps and important information are included.

5. Ask three workers who do not normally do this task to test your procedure.

6. Review their performance.

7. Edit your procedure to ensure it is clear and can be easily understood and implemented by workers who have no experience doing the task.

8. Finalise the procedure and add it to your manual or electronic filing system. Be sure to include a version number and date for review.

9. Show your boss and explain the process.

10. Seek approval to continue creating procedures for all the tasks identified in your Workflow Diagram.

11. Repeat the process for all tasks.

This step completes the 4 Steps To Business Freedom. If you have completed all four assignments, you should now have a clear understanding of your business processes and who does what, when and why. Your procedures are the How.

To recap, your first assignment was to create a Workflow Diagram.

Your second assignment was to use the diagram to create your Functional Organisation Chart, identifying the roles you need now and into the future to carry out the work.

The third step was to create and document Key Performance Indicators and Key Behaviour Indicators for each role within the organisation.

Lastly, using all the information from the Workflow Diagram and Organisation Chart, you created a list of all the tasks that need to be performed. Now it's a matter of using that Table of Contents and writing procedures for each task.

This is the exact process I follow when I consult with businesses across all industries. You now have the process which you can apply in any section in any organisation.

In the next chapter we will look at how you use this process to customise and find solutions specifically for your business.

# SECTION 3

## CUSTOMISE YOUR BUSINESS PROCESSES

Chapter 8

# Use the Process and Customise to Your Organisation

The above four steps are what I use every time I consult with a business to help them streamline their operations. You now have the process. It's not a prescription. I act as a facilitator, not a doctor.

In your role as champion, you are now the facilitator following the process. You know your business and the team know their roles, so it's imperative to ask first and listen before offering suggestions for "better" ways to do things. For example, I wouldn't prescribe a written diary to someone who uses an electronic calendar, but I might suggest some different tools that go with the electronic calendar.

Often, new ideas and ways of doing things will emerge as you go through the steps and assignments above. However, remain silent with your recommendations until you have completed the entire Workflow Diagram.

## Customised Case Studies

Here are a couple of case studies to help you identify how using the process can create a customised solution for your organisation.

*Psychologists Room Booking Procedure*

Prior to working with the team, the admin staff used a complicated spreadsheet system to assign consulting rooms to their team of psychologists. Some psychologists preferred the rooms upstairs. Some preferred the furniture in some rooms. The admin team were totally frustrated, doing their best to accommodate all team members' preferences and ensure the rooms were fully booked.

Listening to the needs of the admin team and the psychologists, I was able to customise a simple solution. We used a whiteboard. We drew a sketch, or mud map as we call it, of the rooms in the building. We asked the psychologists to choose a magnet they wanted to represent themselves. We asked them to place their magnet on the whiteboard in the area that represented the room they intended to use for the day.

The new process was an instant success. The admin team no longer had to worry about scheduling rooms or upsetting psychologists. The psychologists could choose the rooms they wanted to use, and everyone could see whether the rooms were at capacity or not.

In fact, I chuckled to myself when I had a review meeting with one of the directors about four weeks after we completed the project. He immediately went to the whiteboard to find a vacant room, stuck his magnet on the room and off we went for the meeting. Easy! Customised!

*Mortgage Broker and the Floor Trays*

An organised and successful mortgage broker wanted to improve her systems for tracking the progress of customer loans. When I first met with her, I was impressed with her manual systems. They worked. She had trays on the floor around her office for each day of the month. When a client loan progressed to the next stage, she simply moved the file to the next day she was to perform an action for the customer.

The director wanted to streamline the process and we developed an electronic system to track the progress. Since then, she has continually improved her processes and is now paper free in the back end.

## The Showroom Dance

Many of my customers have a sales process for engaging prospective customers. The client who imports kitchens has a showroom with kitchens fully installed, so customers can see some examples to help them create and design their own customised kitchen.

The managing director had a particular sequence he wanted his sales team to follow when showing the display kitchens to prospective customers. He explained the process to me and together we came up with what we called The Showroom Dance.

When a potential customer entered the showroom, a sales representative would greet them and invite them to dance (not literally). The sales representative would ask questions using their customised Enquiry Form and move them gracefully around the showroom from display to display. At the end of the dance, the sales representative had enough information to make a recommendation to the prospective customer and provide a quote. Prior to creating The Showroom Dance, the managing director bore the responsibility for sales. By documenting the dance and training the staff, his business grew rapidly because the business now had more capacity to service more customers.

## Get More Freedom

Every business, business owner and Second-In-Command is unique. What I've found over the years is "you can't see the label from inside the jar". The biggest issue people have is being able to unpack what they know in a format that can be easily communicated to other team members.

The 4 Steps To Business Freedom gives you the process to achieve this and you can complete the assignments at your own pace. How quickly you go is entirely up to you.

*Replacing Yourself*

If you want the freedom to expand your role or the business, you'll need to find a way to replace yourself. An extremely clever husband and wife team grew their educational tour company from scratch. Initially an employed bus driver, he noticed how stressed the school teachers were when it came time to take the children on school excursions to visit Parliament House and other historic places. He convinced his wife to become certified as a travel agent and together they started the business with a limited number of tour buses. He developed a spreadsheet to work out the costs per child for the teachers and she liaised with the teachers to design the tours. When I met them, they had a dream of going sailing but were tied to the business.

Our first task was to document how to cost a tour to be able to create a quote for the teachers. Once we had the documented procedure, we could train one of the team to take over the role. We also created KPIs and KBIs for the role, which ensured the team member knew what she had to do to what standard to succeed in the role. It was an easy handover. Freed from the costing coordinator's role, the wife then used the Organisation Chart to envision her next role as the national marketing manager. She set herself a time frame of six months and a revenue goal which she easily achieved.

A few years later I ran into her at the beach. She and her husband had just returned from a six-month sailing vacation. She had learned the process I used and continued to implement the four steps into her business. Today, she and her husband have employed a general manager. They enjoy time with their grandchildren and, of course, continue to sail.

*Train Your Team*

Sadly, many real estate principals find themselves working almost 24 hours a day, 7 days a week to earn revenue to support the business. This isn't sustainable. The answer lies in being able to train your sales team to achieve the results the principal does. One principal I worked with was initially responsible for bringing in 76% of the entire company revenue. He completed our Leading Yourself and Leading Others experience and engaged in executive coaching with me. He had a goal to have the choice of not having to go to work if he didn't choose to by 55 years of age. He achieved his goal at 54 years and 6 months. He applied himself to training his team, delegating to staff and, as a result, his contribution to the business revenue was reduced to just 6% at the same time he doubled his sales team and their revenue.

You now have the exact process I use. If you get good at your craft, you'll be able to customise your company processes, resulting in more time, money, authority and freedom for yourself, your boss and your team overall.

# Chapter 9
# Promote Yourself

When I was first employed in the franchise organisation, my remuneration started at $40,000. Three years later, this had increased to six figures. I was fortunate my boss recognised my ability and enthusiasm for improving the way we did things. He realised I was an asset to the company and he wanted to retain me. He was an astute leader and manager and understood I was motivated to improve myself, grow and learn. So, he found ways to satisfy my desire to grow (and of course earn more) and I continued to serve the company.

How about you? Is your boss astute or do you need to find ways to promote yourself and your achievements to him? Completing the assignments and sharing your results with your boss should help.

Another way you can do this is to delegate any menial tasks you have, so you can focus on the bigger picture and engage in more strategic work. Delegating will give you capacity which you can offer to your boss.

"Hey boss, I've systemised these procedures and delegated them to this person and that person. With my extra capacity, I've been thinking about the business and wondered what you might think about doing <insert your suggestions>?"

Sharing examples of what you have achieved and how you have invested in creating more time, which you can apply to helping your boss get more time, money and freedom, will ultimately help you to have the same. Don't be shy in sharing what you have done for the company but don't be arrogant about it either.

Simply continue to work your magic. Improve the company operations, improve your own leadership and management skills, and frequently offer more time and solutions to your boss. If she doesn't notice or isn't willing to acknowledge your efforts, you can be assured the competition is watching.

But chances are it will have the opposite effect. In my case, I'd been working on improving systems with a client and training his staff to be leaders within his real estate business for many years.

One day, while travelling in Tasmania as part of our three-year jaunt around the country in an eight-metre motorhome, my client rang.

"Are you still doing systems? It'll be 10-12 hours a week work," he asked.

"Sure, I can help out."

That 12 hours turned into near full-time work, as I worked diligently to set up better systems. But being the typical CVO, he had grander visions. For three years he'd had an idea for another business but hadn't been able to find someone to help set it up.

"Shirl, you understand me, you understand how I work and you can see what I want to do. I know you can help do it," he said.

While he came up with the business idea, he knew he couldn't get it implemented without me. So, we partnered up on the project.

Within six months we had it set up. Our first client started with us on Christmas Day – despite me still figuring out the systems. And now, it's on track to make $5 million within 18 months.

**Joining The Dots**

By now, you should realise your value. You've implemented the four steps, you've made money and time reappear, and you may be wondering what's next?

Consulting to business owners and team leaders over the years, I've found when I completed a project helping them to streamline their operations, the new systems were at risk of not being implemented because they didn't know how to lead and manage their people. As a result, I continued to work with them on an individual basis as an executive coach, while delivering leadership and communication skills training programs for their teams.

Being able to communicate clearly and hold your team accountable are skills that can be learned and improved. The following are areas you can consider for the next phase of your development:

1. Leadership skills
2. Interpersonal communication skills
3. Strategic thinking
4. Becoming a visionary
5. Networking skills
6. Train-the-trainer skills
7. Personal development (increased self-awareness).


If you want to take this further and have access to me twice a month, then consider joining the Practical Leaders Membership program or the Leading Yourself and Leading Others experience. For more information, go to https://shirleydalton.com/2IC.

In the meantime, I congratulate you for stepping up and developing not only yourself but the organisation and its workers. You have now earned those stripes on your loyal lieutenant's jacket. Wear them with pride.

PS. I love feedback and questions. You are welcome to contact me directly with any questions, feedback, case studies and results at shirley@shirleydalton.com.

# About The Author

Shirley Dalton is a business and leadership expert, speaker and author. She is also the creator of the Blueprint For Business Freedom and a leading authority on proven profitable processes. Her teachings demonstrate how blending people, processes and possibilities can help business owners and team leaders create their ideal business lifestyle to avoid burnout and their personal and business lives working against them.

Over 30 years, Shirley has helped thousands of business owners and employees around the world release lifelong limiting beliefs, put in place solid systems and procedures, as well as develop and improve their leadership skills.

Shirley helps business owners, leaders and managers to get their businesses under control and grow themselves and their teams so the business works for them and their teams giving them more money, more time and less stress.

She has degrees in psychology and education, and has invested hundreds of thousands of dollars and travelled the world learning from the best. However, ultimately, she just wants to help you be, do, have and feel what you want. Her clients' success is her success and there is an abundance of this.

Her expertise has yielded incredible results for her clients. As the COO for an Australian international franchise organisation, she streamlined the systems to enable the company to list on the Australian Stock Exchange and grow from around 200 franchises to 550 worldwide – with just 17 employees. She also provided coaching and mentoring to the franchisees and master franchisees globally.

She restructured the appointment system for a financial planner who then doubled the size of their business and revenue without adding any extra time or staff.

These are just some of the many clients she's mentored to achieve their dreams.

Shirley can help provide the information and guidance to help you grow your business, better lead your people, improve your mindset and get your time back.

Shirley loves travelling and lives in Newcastle in New South Wales with her husband Ross.